THE TOURISM SCHOOL

PREFACE

Welcome to *Practical Guide to Everyday Air Ticketing*—a concise, easy-to-use resource designed to provide you with step wise procedure on how to issue Air Tickets on GDS Amadeus at lowest fare with ancillary services demand by travellers. This guide is an excellent way of understanding Air Ticketing on GDS Amadeus for a Travel Aspirant who wishes to work in Travel Industry or upgrade your skillset .Whether you are seasoned travel agent or just starting your journey to become one, this guide aims to help you with practical solutions and insights, offering quick references and actionable advice in a portable format.

Second part of the guide distils answers to 100 questions which every Air Ticketing professional may have in mind before/after issuing airline ticket helping you solve problems and take quick actions

We hope this guide will empower you to work smarter, not harder, and that it will serve as a reliable resource whenever you need it. May this guide support your success and continuous learning.

Sarosh Kinger

This Practical Guide consists of 2 parts

Part 1

In this section, guide focuses on step wise procedure with description and commands on how to issue air ticket on GDS Amadeus. It also covers changes which reflect in your booking before & after command is processed

Issuing basic return E-Ticket is a 20 step procedure

Guide covers 10 steps on how to add free and chargeable ancillary services as per demand by travellers,

3 steps on how to communicate with the airlines & 2 steps on how to Void, Cancel/Refund the E Ticket

Guide also helps the reader to understand timelines issued by Airline & how to interpret replies by Airlines & take appropriate action.

Part 2

In this section, guide answers 100 questions in the form of Frequent Asked Questions (FAQs) which Air Ticketing Professional may come across.

Index

A PNR contains details of Passenger' reservation and other information related to Passenger's trip. PNR can also contain information to assist airline with passenger handling.

Information inserted in PNR is called an element and is assigned a Line No. A PNR can have maximum of 999 elements. Out of 999, five elements are mandatory and rest are optional.

These 5 Mandatory elements are

P R I N T

To start PNR creation in command mode, you must know the codes of origin city and destination city.

Proceed further for step wise procedure from Decoding Encoding till Ticket issuance.

STEPS	DESCRIPTION	COMMANDS
Step 1	Decode Departure & Arrival City /Airport Name Decode Airline Code	*DAN DEL ; DAN NYC;* *DNA Lufthansa*
Step 2	Display Availability/Schedule for particular date for a city pair *(for particular Airline for specific Cabin - Economy)*	AN10JANDELNYC/ALH/KM
Step 3	Sell seats in the class mentioned in the last for lowest available fare *(sell 2 seas in K class for airline mentioned at line no 1)*	SS2K1
Step 4A	Add Return using shortcut *(follow up command if Availability is displayed as last output)* or Add Return by displaying fresh availability command	ACR25JAN AN25JANNYCDEL/ALH/KM
Step 4B	Sell Seats in lowest available Class for lowest fare *(no of seats sold should be same for all the flight segments in PNR as PNR will not be saved)*	SS2K1
Step 5	Add Names of Passengers *(Should be taken for Passport only) . Adding Tag is optional in case of Adult as system assumes without tag passenger as an Adult Passenger*	NM1 KINGER/SAROSH MS(ADT) NM1 KINGER/ KAMLESH MS (ADT/29JAN67)
Step 6	Add Phone Element – Add Contact Detail of Travel Agent	AP
Step 7	Add Contact Detail of Passengers – Phone No Add Contact Detail of Passengers – Email Id *(Step 7 is Optional ,Contact Details mentioned here is not transmitted to Airline)*	AP DEL 9899774407/P1 APE SAROSH@GMAIL.COM

Step 8	Add Ticketing Element – *if No Time Limit is Required Or else* Add Time Limit with date and/or time *(if Time Limit is added PNR will show as actionable PNR in Queue)*	TKOK TKTL05JAN/1600
Step 9	Add Reference *(Name of person working on the PNR)*	RF MISA
Step 10	End Transaction & Retrieve the PNR	ER
Itinerary	To Display Itinerary To email itinerary to email id in AP To email itinerary to any other email id	IBD/IED IEP-EMLA IEP-EMLA-sarosh@gmail.com

Important Note: On saving, PNR No / Record Locator will get generated.If record locator is not generated in maximum 12 hrs. time, travel agent must contact airline.

Itinerary will remain active until last ticketing date and time mentioned in OPW/OPC element *(received by Airline).*

OPW/OPC will mention the time limit issued by Airline to hold the itinerary. Travel Agent must add fares to issue the ticket or release the seats before the time limit issued by airline. If time limit issued by Airline is not followed then itinerary will get cancelled automatically.

Refer to the Appendix-I to understand how to read replies by Airlines

<table>
<tr><td colspan="3" align="center">ADD FARES TO YOUR BOOKING</td></tr>
<tr><td>Step 11</td><td>Check the fare of the class you are holding
(if there is single fare, directly ticket image will be displayed)

Convert booking class to lowest possible available fare class</td><td>FXX

FXR</td></tr>
<tr><td>Step 12</td><td>Check the ticket Image of lowest Fare displayed to see baggage offered & Tax Breakdown
(if list of fares is displayed)</td><td>FQQ line no</td></tr>
<tr><td>STEP 13</td><td>Save the fare permanently -it saves the PNR till last Fare ticketing date
-if there is single fare, it will automatically get saved on doing FXP
-in case multiple fares exist ,if you wish same fare for both the passengers
-in case of multiple fares, when you wish different fare for both passengers
On saving fare with FXP, TST will get created. This is transitional stored ticket record. To open TST.</td><td>FXP

FXT2/P1,2

FXT2/P1//3/P2

TQT</td></tr>
<tr><td>STEP 14</td><td>Add Reference & save PNR</td><td>RFMISA;ER</td></tr>
</table>

On saving Fare, 3 changes will reflect in PNR.

- *TST tag will appear on the tagline of PNR*
- *FE element (Fare Endorsement element) appears in PNR*
- *FV element (Fare Validating element , This has airline code on which ticket will get issued)*

Important Note:

Non adherence to OPW/OPC time limit received by Airline will result in cancellation of itinerary post the time limit mentioned in OPW/OPC leading to fare becoming Invalid.

Fare is guaranteed till last ticketing date mentioned in TST/Ticket Image. Ensure to issue the ticket taking into consideration the earliest ticketing time limit.

99% times earliest time limit will be the automated time limit (ATL) issued by airline in OPW/OPC

CHECKLIST BEFORE ISSUING TICKET. ENSURE THAT

- Action codes of all flight segments are confirmed i.e HK, if not agent must take appropriate action.

- TST is saved, confirmed & autopriced

- OPC date is valid

- Form of Payment is handy for IATA Go Lite Users

  (Go Standard can issue ticket on Cash/Invoice for payment through BSP)

Ticket can be issued same day or anytime later before fare last ticketing date and airline time limit, post which class may become unavailable and fares are subject to change.

Step 15	Add Mandatory Fare Remarks required to Issue Ticket Fare Validating Element (FV) Form of Payment Element (FP) Fare Commission Element (FM)	FV is automatically added with TST creation FP FM1 (means 1%)
Step 16	**Ticket is ready to be issued.** *If system warns for APIS/SFPD or SRCTCM/SRCTCE details then details must be entered else ticket will not issue.* *In such cases, Step 17 & 18 should be followed before Step 16.*	TTP
Step 17	To add APIS To add SFPD	SRDOCS AI HK1-P-IND-N675435-IND-10JAN86-F-28NOV30-KINGER-SAROSH MS/P1 SRDOCS AI HK1-----10JAN86-F--KINGER-SAROSH MS/P1
Step 18	Transmit Contact Details to Airline Transmit Phone No Transmit Email id *(Only 1 is mandatory)*	SRCTCM-9899774407/P1,2 SRCTCE-SAROSH//GMAIL.COM/P1
Step 19	Ticket is ready to be issued	TTP
Step 20	To display E Ticket Record *In PNR Mode* *Outside PNR*	 TWD RTTKT/13 DIGIT TICKET NO
Step 21	To email Itinerary Receipt To email address mentioned in AP element To any other email address	 ITR-EMLA ITR-EML-sarosh@gmail.com

On Issuing ETKT, 5 changes take place in the PNR

- *FA element with ticket number, amount, currency, date of ticket issuance appears in PNR*
- *FB element with Amadeus Interface record is added in PNR*
- *Ticketing element gets changed to TKOK (if it was on TL earlier)*
- *FM line gets updated*
- *Sales gets recorded*

Once ticket is issued, following elements cannot be cancelled.

- *Name cannot be cancelled. Can be only modified with/without resissuance*
- *FA element cannot get cancelled*

Important Note:

Ticket can be voided on same day it was issued without any cancellation charges.

If Ticket is cancelled after midnight of day ticket was issued, Cancellation Charges as per fare note will apply.

If ticket is cancelled in No Show window, which usually starts 24hrs before departure for most of the airlines, No show Charges will apply along with cancellation charges.

There are 2 ways to add Extra Baggage:

First , Open Catalogue of services by using FXK command and move to step 28 directly. *FXK entry does not work TST is not stored.* If baggage cannot be added from here then

Second method is to follow Steps from 22 to 30

ADDING EXTRA BAG		
Step 22	Display List of EMD services offered by Airline	EGSD/VLH *(LH is airline code)*
Step 23	There are multiple Baggage Codes. Note the code of Additional/Extra Baggage	*Retrieve PNR & Add* SRMBAG-10kgs/P1 *(For 10 kg additional Baggage)*
Step 24	To check the price of Extra Baggage *(price will show once service has been confirmed by Airline as HK status code)*	FXH
Step 25	To save the price of Extra Baggage	FXG
Step 26	TSM will get created *(TSM stands for Transitional Stored Miscellaneous Services)* To open TSM	TQM

Step 27	Add Form of Payment *(add it manually or it is easier to select Form of payment by scrolling down the TSM)*	TMI/FP-CCCAxxxxxxx/XDDMM/CODE (CA is credit card code, xxx… is credit card number, / Xis followed expiry date/ one time use approval code by bank in
Step 28	Reference & Save is must to save last action Issued *EMD (if ticket is already issued)* Issue ETKT and EMD together	RFMISA;ER TTM TTP/TTM

Step 29	*Display EMD*
	   -In PNR mode
	   - Outside PNR
		
		EWD
		EWD/EMD document no

Step 30	To email EMD To email address mentioned in AP element To any other email address	 EPR-EMLA EPR-EML-sarosh@gmail.com

To issue ETKT, EMD, Email Itinerary, ITR, EPR to email id mentioned in AP in single command

TTP/TTM/IEP-EMLA/ITR-EMLA/EPR-EMLA

Important Note:

Like ETKT, EMD can be voided on same day it was issued without any cancellation charges.

COMMUNICATION WITH AIRLINES

To start any type of communication with the Airlines, ensure that PNR no/Record Locator of Airline has been received in the PNR. If PNR is not received within 24 hrs of PNR Creation, airline must be contacted.

SSR means Special Service Request. All types of SSR have specific codes. Request to Airlines should be made through codes. Airline will reply back with the action code which should be interpreted correctly by travel agent. Hence this is a two way communication method, from Travel Agent to Airline & vice versa.

OSI means Other Service Information. Any communication which does not consist of SSR code can be made to airlines through OSI. This is one way form of communication from travel to airline only.

OSI & SSR can be added prior to ticket issuance or after ticket issuance. Ensure to add at least 72 hrs before departure so as to give time to airline to reply for your request.

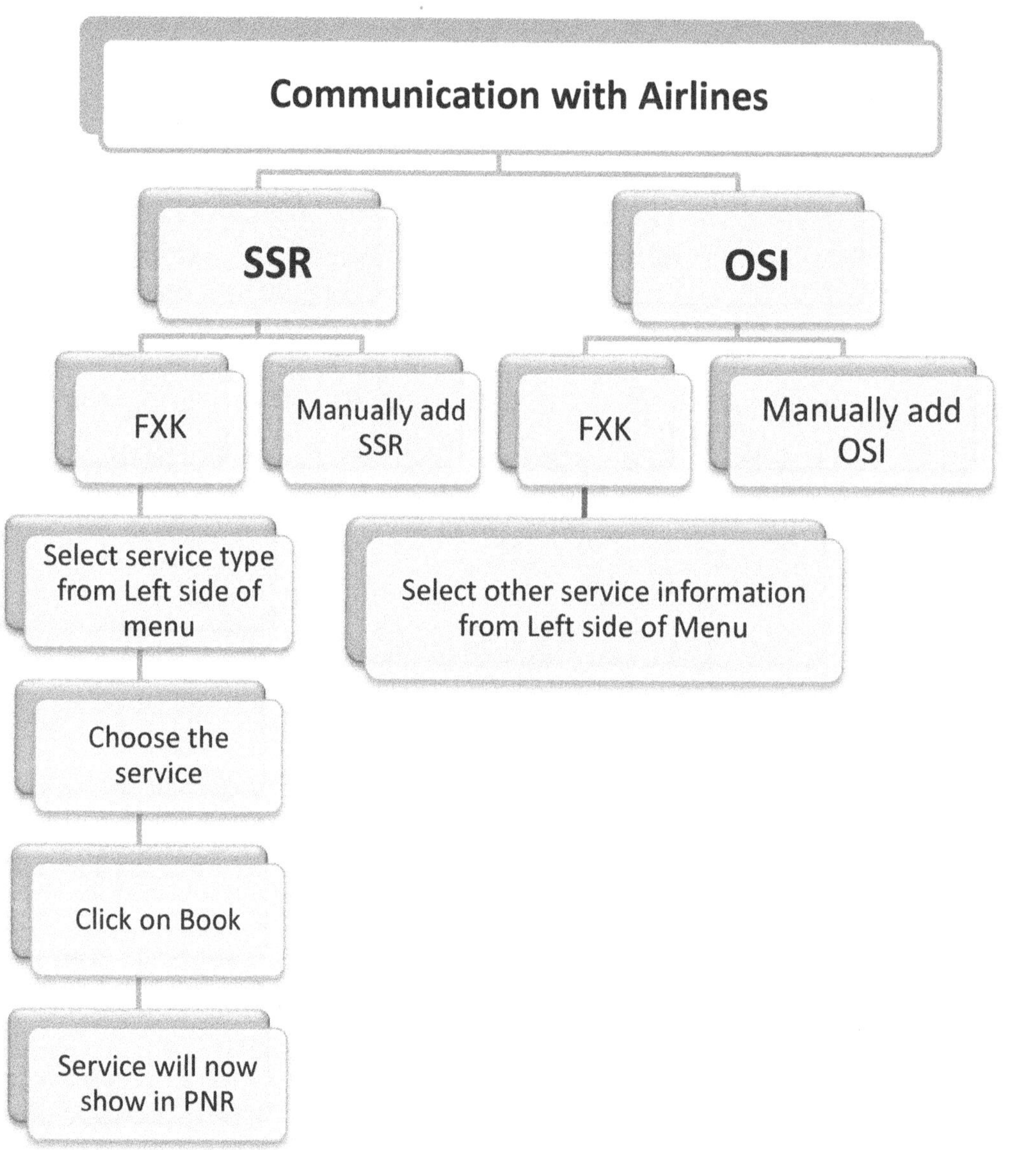

Communication with Airlines
SSR
OSI
FXK
Manually add SSR
FXK
Manually add OSI
Select service type from Left side of menu
Select other service information from Left side of Menu
Choose the service
Click on Book
Service will now show in PNR

Second Method	**MANUAL ADDITION OF OSI/SSR**	
Step 31	Adding OSI	OS LH pax 1 has fracture in leg OS YY pax 1 has fracture in leg *(airline code for specific airline* *or* *yy to send same message to all* *airlines in PNR)*
STEP 32	Adding SSR -Meal Request -Special Service Request -Special Service Request -Seat Preference	SRHNML/P1 *(meal request for* *pax 1)* SRWCHR/P1 *(wheelchair* *request for pax 1)* SRMAAS – VIP passengers/P1,2 ST/W/P1 *(SM command can be used to* *display Seat map)*
STEP 33	Add Reference & Save your PNR *(to save last actions performed by* *Travel Agent)*	RFMISA;ER

Changes in PNR after SSR/OSI are added

OSI does not receive reply from Airline hence no action is required to be taken by Travel Agent

Once SSR is added in PNR & PNR is saved, SSR will be get reply from Airline in same line as action code. Action code consist of 2 alphabets followed by no of pax who wish that particular service.

It is important for Travel Agent to interpret action code and take appropriate action.

Important Note:

To see list of SSR codes, use system help HE SSR

To understand replies by Airline and appropriate action to be taken, refer to Appendix – I

Once ticket is issued, any changes in ETKT is possible only of coupon is

Either **O** (open)

Or   **A** (Airport Control)

Few airlines may not allow doing changes even with status A especially if changes are requested 24 hrs before departure time

Post Ticket Issuance steps are standalone steps on need basis.

VOID		
Step 34	To Void the ETKT or EMD	TRDC

Changes in PNR & ETKT after Voiding ETKT

In PNR, ET in FA element gets converted to EV

In ETKT , coupon status changes to V

FULL REFUND		
Step 35 A - FULL REFUND WITH PENALTY FOR UNUSED TICKET	To cancel ETKT with penalty amount 10000 INR *(System automatically assumes currency of ticket issuance)*	Either use TRF/13 digit ticket no./FULL/CP100000A Or *follow 3 step procedure* TRF/13 digit ticket no TRFU/CP10000 TRFP
Step 35B- FULL REFUND WITH WAIVER CODE	To cancel ETKT with Waiver Code 456789	TRF/13 digit ticket no/FULL TRFU/Rcancellation_by_airline *(remarks are optional, space is not allowed in remarks)* TRFU/WA456789 *(WAfollowed by code no space)* TRFP

Changes in PNR & ETKT after refund is processed.

In PNR, ET in FA element gets converted to ER

In ETKT , coupon status changes to R

Part-II
FREQUENTLY ASKED QUESTIONS
(100 FAQ's)

1.   Who is Child Passenger in Air Ticketing? How to add Child Entry in PNR?

Child is a passenger who is 2 years old and has not celebrated 12th birthday as on date of travel .

Tag of CHD needs to be entered in name element for Child Discount. Salutation of male child is MSTR (master) and salutation of female child is MISS (miss).

Format to make entry of child passenger is:

Example: NM1 ARORA/AARAV MSTR (CHD/29JAN16)

Example: NMI ARORA/AARTI MISS (CHD/29JAN16)

2.   How to add Infant without Seat?

Infant is a passenger who has not celebrated 2nd birthday as on date of travel.

Infant can travel 2 ways – Without Seat or With Seat

Without seat, which means seat is not purchased for Infant and infant will travel in the lap of Adult passenger. Hence name entry is done in the tag.

Example: Example: NM1   KINGER/SAROSH   MS   (INF   ARORA/AARAV MSTR/29JAN25)

Where Sarosh is an adult and Aarav is an infant

With Seat , which means seat is purchased for Infant. In this case, Infant needs to be entered like Child Passenger but tag will be INS although CHD can also be used.

Example: NM1 ARORA/AARAV MSTR (INS/29JAN25)
Salutation of male child is MSTR (master) and salutation of female child is MISS(miss).

3.   What is the minimum age of Infant to travel for International Airline?
Infant as old as 2 days can travel in case if urgent need to travel however most of the Airlines have a policy of healthy born infant to be atleast 7 days old to travel (in case the infant is less than 7 days, fit to travel certificate from infant's paedtrician as well as physician of medical department of specific airline is mandatory)

4.   What %age of discount Child & Infant Passenger can expect in Airline Ticketing?
Child gets minimum discounts of 0% maximum discount of 25% .
Infant without seat gets 90% discount & Infant with seat is treated similar to Child passenger

5. Would pricing method remain same when Child and Infant exist in the PNR?

Yes the pricing method & commands remains same . TSTs created are directly propotional to the types of passengers in PNR. All adults will be part of one TST, all children will be part of another TST and so on.

For example: if there are 2 adults, 1 chd and 1 infant in PNR. There will be 3 TST, first TST will consist of 2 adults, second TST will consist of child and third TST will consist of Infant passenger.

6. If Infant becomes Child in Transit , What is the best method way to book ?

Ideally Infant should be priced as Child passenger for the entire journey however there are few airlines who favour by giving free seat on return journey to Infant turning Child in transit. You may add OSI element/SSR check in element (SSRCKIN – free flow text) in PNR to inform the airline for the same. All the approvals, etc must be made before start of the journey (ideally 72 hrs prior to departure) to avoid last minute hassle.

7. Can Infant be added later, after ticket issuance of Adult & Child?

Yes definitely, Infant without seat can be added even after ticket for other passengers has been issued. As TST of infant without seat will be separate, hence ensure to issue TST of Infant passenger only in this case.

For example if TST no of Infant is T3 then to attach ticket of infant passenger in same PNR. Just issue infant ticket using entry TTP/T3

8. *Can infant travel with guardians (who are not parents to infant)?*

Yes, Infant can travel with guardians with the below mentioned documents which are must in this case

- First, Consent letter from parents approving travel of infant with guardians
- Second, Passport copy or ID proof of Parents
- Third, Relationship proof of Guardians with infant
- Fourth, death certificate of parents , if parents are deceased
- Original Passport or Id may be asked at airport to verify signatures of parents on consent letter.

9. *Can meals or seat request be added after ticket is issued?*

Yes, special services can be added anytime once PNR number of airline has been generated. Ensure to add atleast 72 hrs before departure to avoid request being rejected.

10. *If I made error in spelling of passenger, is it possible to edit/modify the name?*

If ticket has not been issued, modification can be attempted in GDS. Not at all airlines allow for the same.

If ticket has been issued, SRCKIN-free flow text can be inserted in PNR to inform Airlines for error in spelling of name. Almost all airlines allow SRCKIN element for

errors in spelling uptil 2 alphabets. Or else get in touch with airline to get the name modified (uptil 2- 3 alphabets only) free of cost.

11. *How many passengers can be added in a single booking?*

Generally 9, few airlines have a limitation of 8 like Emirates (EK). Codeshare airlines allow either 7 or 4 . You may check the same in Amadeus by using command HE ETT Airline code , from output choose the follow command which shows data for Indian market(IN)

12. Are there any extra charges to be paid, if form of payment credit card is used?

Yes , few airlines charge extra fee for credit card payments which gets reflected as OB Fee and needs to be paid as EMD .

13. I don't want to use credit card form of payment, What are the other options available?

Scroll down the TST to see forms of payment allowed for you or else you check using command

HE ETT airline code , from output choose the follow command which shows data for Indian market(IN)

14. Can I use more than one payment mode for ticket issuance?

Yes, you can. 3 form of payment options are allowed per TST

15. I did not receive PNR No by Airline, how long should I wait in such case?

Not more than 24 hrs. After 24 hrs, you must contact airline. If travel date is within 24 hrs , you may contact airline after waiting for 15 mins.

16. I did not follow OPW/OPC date & itinerary in PNR shows HX, What does it mean? What am I supposed to do in this case?

Holding HX segment will attract penalty by Airline. Ideally, you should remove the same within 24 -48 hrs.

17. In the above case, is it possible to Resell the itinerary and Re Price it ?

Yes, you can Resell, Reprice.

18. Now I see lowest class if available, Can I change the booking class in my PNR to lowest class ?

Till ticket has not been issued, yes you can do any changes in PNR. Once ticket is issued, degrading to lower class may not benefit as you would need to reissue/revalidate the ticket with/without penalty according to fare rule.

19. In above case, would I get fare difference refunded by Airline?

Airlines do not refund any amount in case class is degraded.

20. One of the passengers in the booking has change in travel plan, ticket has already been issued. Is it possible to make changes for one of the passengers only without affecting other passengers itinerary?

Yes, you can split particular passenger. After split procedure is complete, you can make changes in PNR of particular person and reissue the ticket.

21. If I book connecting flights with different Airlines, do I need to check-in luggage again at connecting point?

If airlines are of same alliance or codeshare partners and ticket is issued on single plating/validating carrier then interline agreement develops on its own ad then there is no need to check-in baggage at connecting point.

22. In case first airline in connecting airline pair gets delayed, would passenger get support for onward journey by airline?

Yes, if ticket was issued on single plating carrier/validating airline.

23. In the above case, my passenger is not willing to wait for long and calls me to make booking on other airline, is it possible to request refund for the onward journey?

Yes, you can inform the airline to arrange travel on other airline citing emergency of passenger or else you may request for waiver code for refund of non-flown segments of itinerary.

24. If first journey in PNR is domestic and onward connecting journey is International, would immigration take at origin or transit point?

Immigration will take place at point from where International journey starts.

25. If any flight segment gets cancelled due to non-adherence to rules, how would I get notified by GDS?

All PNR's which require action show up in Queues. Refer to Appendix –II for queues.

26. Can I issue ticket on Waitlist?

No , ticket cannot be issued on waitlisted. Itinerary can be sold and PNR can be created on waitlist, ticket can be issued only once waitlist is approved by airline.

27. How would I get notified my waitlist itinerary gets confirmed?

It will show up in Queue no 2 . Refer to Appendix –II for queues.

28. Can a child travel alone?

Yes child above the age of 5 years can travel alone as Unaccompanied Minor. Unaccompanied minor does not enjoy child discount and is priced as adult passenger. There is SSR fee of handling of unaccompanied minor which must be added in PNR and issued as EMD.

29. My client is travelling for business purpose and wants GST Invoice. Is it possible to issue GST Invoice? What is the procedure for the same?

SSR for GST must be added in PNR before ticket issuance . To generate ticket and invoice use command TTP/ITD

To email invoice ITD-EML-MBAUER@YKT.COM

30. My passenger is not having last name on Passport, what will be the entry format for the same?

All airlines have different rule in this case. Few airlines would ask you to repeat the first name in last name and other may ask you insert FNU as first name and move the first name to last name .

Airlines like Air India have different name format if you are travelling to Western Hemisphere and different format if you are travelling to UK.

Hence fool proof answer is to check on the website of the airline or call airline for the exact name format

31. Client has already reached airport & now the client is informed that airline has cancelled the reservation. My client has urgent need to travel, If I book some other airline can refund be requested from already scheduled airline in this case and how?

Yes, full refund can be issued provided you take waiver code from the airline. Refer to section of Full Refund to know the process of refund.

32. What is the last timeline to add extra baggage in already issued ticket?

Ideally 72 hrs before departure

33. What is the last time line to add Special Services like Meals, Wheelchair, seats etc in PNR?

Ideally 72 hrs before departure although you may add free services 24 hrs before departure but certain region specific meals like Kosher Meal needs to be requested atleast 72 hrs before departure.

34. My client is pregnant; can she travel for international journey?

Yes definitely. Air Travel is allowed till 36 weeks of healthy pregnancy .After 28 weeks airline may ask to submit fit to travel medical certificate signed by your gynaecologist.

35. Can single parent travel with 2 infants/twins?

Yes , it is mandatory to purchase seat for 1 infant in this case. Few airlines have made it mandatory to travel with car Seat for Infant with seat .

There are airlines in Middle East, Africa which have policy of equal number of adults with infant , hence single parent with 2 infants is not allowed in such airlines.

36. Can waitlist flight segment and confirmed segment remain in same PNR? Would airline cancel one of them because of duplicate segments?

Yes , both can be in same PNR. Airline will cancel one of them only after 24 hrs of waitlist getting confirmed. Airline will allow you time to cancel one of them for 24 hrs post which airline may automatically cancel one of them .

37. I have 2 clients with same name travelling in same PNR, both are different individuals but system warns me for duplicate names? How should I handle this in GDS?

Insert passport details of passengers for validity , SSR CKIN entry . You may still face error, if you do then you would need to contact airline.

38. Is it possible to sell itinerary, check fares and ignore PNR without completing all the steps as I have no intention to create PNR ? Is there any limit imposed by Airline to do so?

You may do so. Most of the airlines allow this uptil 5 times in economy cabin . If repeatedly this is followed in bigger numbers, airline may send you ADM under the category of Churning Violation

39. I am getting quite cheaper fare, Can I hold the PNR on any name right away and change the name later before issuing the ticket? Is it possible to change the complete name after issuing ticket?

No, it is not possible.

40. I need dummy ticket for my client for Visa Filing. Is it possible to issue dummy ticket through GDS without issuing the actual ticket?

Yes you can. IBD/IED commands displays the itinerary which can be used as dummy ticket but not for all the countries of the world.

41. Till when the issued ticket or EMD be Cancelled/Voided in GDS without any cancellation charges?

On same day only under BSP

42. What is the last timeline to cancel the issued ticket to avoid No Show Charges?

Ticket goes into No Show Clause 24 hrs before departure for most of the airlines. Hence , ticket should be cancelled before the no show clause to avoid no show charges.

43. I issued a ticket which is partially refundable, till when can I request for refund through GDS?

Till ticket record can be displayed, you can request refund.

44. My client is travelling by connecting airlines, he wants to book Extra Luggage .On which airline to book extra luggage?

Luggage should be booked on most significant carrier. Read the rules of most significant carrier for the same, you may check the same website of the airline.

45. I wish to issue ticket for Air India but system prompts me as" No Ticketing Authority" although I have made PNR filed fares. Why I am not able to issue ticket?

It means you have selling right and ticketing rights are not been issued to you. Kindly check with your GDS or else you would need to do capping to take ticketing authority.

46. Family member of my client has deceased, can I request for refund in this case if my client does not wish to travel?

Yes you can within 45 days of death on providing the death certificate.

47. Family member of my client is critically unwell and is on ventilator and my client is at international destination, Can I pre-pone & rebook ticket of my client without any charges?

Ideally yes, provided you can show the document stating the health of the passenger and relationship certificate. On showing document, either Airline can change itinerary on your behalf and reissue it or else Airline can issue you waiver code to reissue without charges.

48. I am not getting good connecting airline pair as per requirement of my client. Can I sell flight segments separately in same single PNR? How would I ensure baggage handling agreement will get created?

You can sell segments separately, ensure 3 things

- Minimum connecting time should be maintained at connecting point
- Airlines should be of same alliance/codeshare
- Ticket should be issued as through ticket on one single airline

If all the above 3 provisions are met, then baggage handling agreement will get created.

49. My client reached airport late and was denied entry at airport? Is travel agent having any control over this, how can I help my client in this regard?

No, you need to check for the reasons why client was not allowed to enter.

Ideally if ticket is issued properly and client reaches airport on time, entry should not have been stopped.

50. Would airline warn me through notification in case I hold duplicate flight segments or cancel one of them by themselves?
Yes in Queue no 97 Category of Dupe Check.

51. Is there any time limit to generate ETKT related documents line Invoice, itinerary? I did not generated at the time of ticket issuance but I need now.
You can print an ITR when you issue an e-ticket or as a separate document, up to 7 days after the issuance or as long as it is active, depending on your market.

52. Is it possible to generate Sales Reports from Amadeus for the month which is passed?
Yes, TJQ entry with filter or date of month can be used

53. Can travel agent make group bookings in Amadeus?
Yes, for the airline which allow. Not all airlines allow group bookings in GDS. It is recommended to contract with the airlines for group bookings & get authorisation for creation & issuance of ticket for group bookings.

54. What is considered as group booking in GDS?

More than 9 passengers in one booking is considered as group booking in GDS.

55. What is difference in group and bulk fare?

Group fare is fixed departure fare, it means all the passengers in the group needs to travel on same fixed departure date

On the other hand , Bulk fare means fare which is purchased in bulk in advance from the airline and sold on individual basis. It has validity and travel date restrictions but it is not fixed departure fare.

56. Airline has replied with status code of UC in flight segment . What should be done in this case?

Filght segments with HX,NO,UC as airline replies should be removed from the airline ideally within 24 hrs- 72 hrs of status appearing on your itinerary else your PNR may attract ADM(penalty)

57. Airline has replied with status code of UC in SSR . What should be done in this case?

Ideally, element contacting UC should be removed from PNR and new SSR can be added. IN SSR's as system doesn't get affect with HX,NO,UC to a greater extent hence removing particular SSR element & adding new SSR can be done even when 72 hrs are left for departure of flight segment in PNR.

58. I am making PNR on Emirates, system is not allowing to sell 9 seats in single PNR although I am able to add 9 passengers in single PNR for LH, LX, BA.
Emirates don't allow 9 passengers in single booking /PNR. To check how many passengrs , airline is allowing in single ONR, use command HE ETT airline code

59. Why in codeshare flights, system does not allow to sell 9 seats in single PNR?
Yes, there is restriction. In Codeshare flight, maximum passengers allowed in single PNR has a limit of 7, however few codeshares may not allow more than 4

60. How many flight segments can be added in Single PNR ?
15 OW and 16 RT

61. How many flight segments can be priced together?
Same as above

62. *I have made PNR on airline website but I would like to issue through GDS , Is it possible?*

Yes its possible. Request airline to provide you edit and ticket extended security (ES) , once it is done you can claim the PNR . Once PNR is claim, you can edit, issue it.

63. *I have made PNR on Galileo but I would like to issue through Amadeus, Is it possible?*

Yes it is possible. Provide edit and ticket extended security (ES) for that particular PNR on Galileo using command *ES/G followed by Amadeus Office Id*

Once it is done you can claim the PNR using RO airline code PNR No of airline Once PNR is claimed, you may use the same.

64. *Do all the airlines allow to sell seat in Waitlist?*
No, all the airlines do not allow to sell seat on waitlist.

65. *How to identify if Airline is allowing to sell seat on Waitlist or not?*
You can check if airline is allowing to sell seat on waitlist or not by using command HE ETT airline code

66. Do we get special fares for Student, Senior Citizens in GDS?

Yes, you need to use correct passenger type code with the name element and system will show the discounted fare by default. Sometimes fare is not cheap directly but is discounted by extra baggage and relaxed fare rules.

67. What is NDC?

NDC stands for New Distribution Capability , it is a graphical interactive easy to understand and act interface used by airline to distribute and sell flight content.

68. Can I see NDC Fare of Airlines on GDS?

Yes, you can

 Although Amadeus has allowed me access of NDC content of few airlines but I wish to see content of other airlines as well for the airlines I am authorised under my IATA? How can I request NDC fare of those airlines?

For airlines which don't show up by default, either speak with your Amadeus Relationship manager for access or get in touch with airlines which demand for agreement for access. For these airlines,you need to sign an agreement for NDC content on your PCC/Office Id. Few airlines may ask for bank guarantee amount for access whereas others may allow you NDC content just with the agreement.

69. My client has a frequent flyer card of Air India? On which all airlines his Air India loyalty frequent flyer card will remain valid.

You can check frequent flyer agreement with command VFFD followed by Airline Code to see list of airlines which have frequent flyer agreement with Air India

70. My client wish to redeem frequent flyer earned miles/points to pay for flight? How can I do that?

FFRairline code – frequent flyer card no./pax no

71. In reference to the above question for codeshare journey, Who would authorise the redemption of miles/points – operating airline or issuing airline?

Operating airline authorises the redemption of points

72. My client's sister has miles/points in her frequent flyer card, can my client (who is not the owner of that card) redeem miles/points of his sister's card?

Yes, it is possible. Entry is FFRairline code – frequent flyer card no.- card holder name/pax no

73. What is Purge? When doesPNR gets purged?

Purge means removal of PNR from the GDS system after a certain period of time. Purged PNR cannot be recovered.

In Amadeus, PNR gets purged after 4 days of last segment being flown.

74. I need to keep PNR live, can I delay the Purge process?

Yes you can by adding Retention Line. PNR will remain live and visible till the date mentioned in retention Line

Example : RU1AHK1DEL10FEB/keep pnr live

(where HK is action code 1 means no. of passengers in PNR, DEL from where services need to be used followed by date till when PNR will remain live)

75. Can past date record be retrieved in Amadeus?

Yes it can be retrieved uptil 3 years after the last segment is completed but in read mode only.

76. I am unable to retrieve the ticket date, my PNR seems purged and unable to retrieve it with past date retrieval method? Can I get ticket data somehow?

Yes only ITR can be displayed or emailed. Use *command ITRD/TKTticketno to email*

77. My PNR is not getting saved, its shows error " Passenger/Segment Association needed"

This error is shown by system when number of passengers added in Booking File/PNR are either more in number or less in number than the no. of seats sold in itinerary

78. My PNR displays warning message "Check Segment Continuity " Should I bypass the warning or take action?

You may bypass the warning if you wish to. This error shows in case of Destination Open Jaws journey. To remove this warning you need to add Surface Segment arrival unknown .

Command for the same is SIARNK

79. What does warning message " check OSI/SSR Codes" mean?

It means there are replies by Airlines for SSR requested by you. Hence you should check the same and take appropriate action.

80. I received warning of " Verify itinerary" . What should I check and how should I verify itinerary?

This warning shows up when there is reply by the airline in the itinerary/flight segments and airline wants you to take action & reconfirm the same then

81. I am pricing flight segments but system displays "Entry not allowed in NHP Conditions " again and again. What could be the error in PNR?

NHP means Non Homogenous Condition. This error is shown by system when number of passengers added in Booking File/PNR are either more in number or less in number than the no. of seats sold in itinerary

82. Can number of seats be modified in PNR ?

Yes possible only till PNR number is not generated although few married segments restrict the same. Once PNR number is generated, no. of seats cannot be changed.

*83. During pricing why do I get this error " ** ATTN** SEG not rebooked Reprice"*

The flight segment becomes unavailable during the rebooking process

There is a discrepancy between the airline's inventory and the availability displayed in Amadeus

84. Why I am not able to make changes to married segments separately?

When married segment control exist on connecting pair, then you need to make changes to both the segments together

85. I am trying to issue ticket but system prompts "Unable to process". Why does system display this message?

It means office profile is not set for ticket issuance for that airline which can be checked by PV/C or else contact Amadeus Help desk

86. How to know list of airlines I am authorised to issue ticket ?

PV/C will display your office profile,restrictions and authorisations.

87. Client reached me to reissue ticket made by other travel agent? Can I claim ticket in my GDS to process reissue?

No, you should not claim until Airline or system where it was originally made has provided you extended security to modify the same .

88. Do airlines give commission on each and every ticket issued through GDS?

Yes but not all the airlines

89. Can travel Agent check the commission amount applicable before Issuing Ticket?

Yes definitely it can be checked by using entry TQT/FM

90. Can Travel Agent pay Net Fare to the Airline after subtracting the eligible commission?

Yes you can by adding Commission element correctly, if system recalculates the amount to be paid .

91. What are CAT 35 fares?

CAT 35 is a category which specifies the conditions related to Negotiated and private fares. If you negotiate fare with the airline the on using NET REMIT

CODE /PRIVATE TOUR CODE special discounts gets applied on your fare. In Fare rule, conditions for the same can be read under Category no 35.

92. For Group bookings made in GDS, can I transmit names of passengers 24 hrs before departure

Ideally, names should be transmitted 72 hrs prior to departure in GDS.

93. I am using GDS system of India; can I issue ticket in Dirhams (AED) currency?

Yes , you can . Ensure to hold the fare in AED currency

94. Do Air Tickets have any validity period?

Yes, it is generally one year from date of issuance.

95. What does validity of Air Tickets signify?

Validity means that ticket should be used and travel must be completed within one year of issuance of ticket.

96. What is Open Ticket? Do open tickets carry any validity period?

Open tickets are flexible airline ticket with no fixed date of travel. Passengers can choose their travel date within the set frame accordingly to the validity & travel range conditions of open ticket.

97. What is the deadline to process refund for the ticket in GDS?

Sales Data in Amadeus is stored for 180 days, if data is available you may process automatic or manual refunds easily. If data is no longer available, you need to create blank refund record then enter details for refund appropriately to process refund.

98. Can refund processed be cancelled, ticket be restored?

Yes on same day. Not at all the airlines allow this in GDS. If airlines does not allow in GDS, you need to contact airline and get it done from airline directly.

99. I contracted with the airlines and Airline gave me a Tour Code under the category of CAT 35? Where this Tour code needs to be mentioned?

Tour Code needs to be mentioned in TST under the tour code option or you may use command FT followed by Tour Code

100.   What is an ADM?

ADM stands for Auto Debit Memo which is penalty imposed by airline for violations made by Travel Agent in Airline Ticketing. For list of violations and reason of issuance of ADM, please refer to website of specific Airline.

101.   I need to book connecting Airline, for one of the flight segment I am not getting lower class in Amadeus but lower class for same routing is available in Galileo, Can I create PNR in Galileo, then transfer it claim it in Amadeus and add other segment from here and then issue ticket.

No, this is system abuse and you may attract ADM due to tampering with availability.

AIRLINE REPLIES

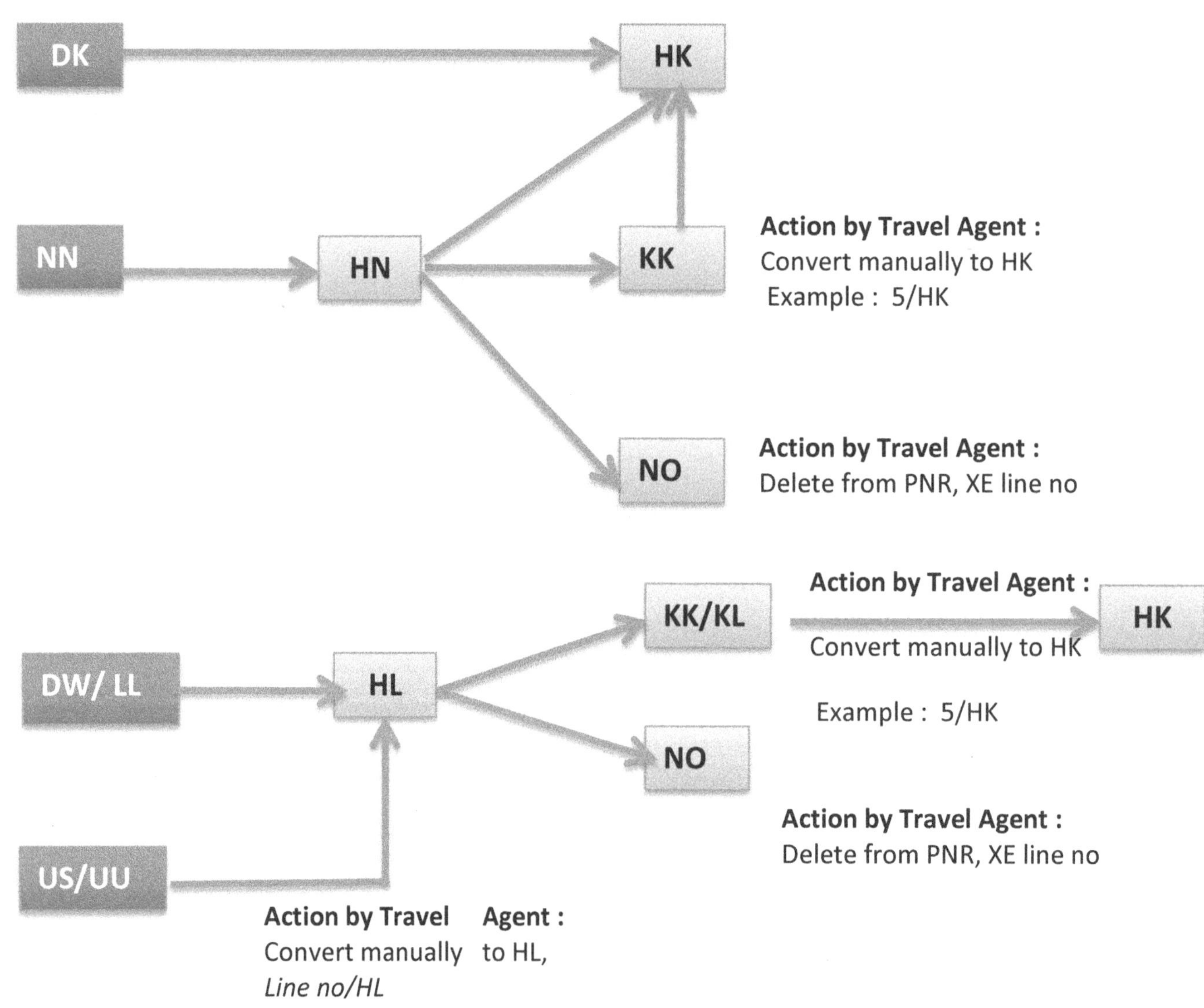

Action by Travel Agent :

Delete element/line no from PNR ideally within 24 hrs of status received from Airline or at last 72 hrs before the departure.

QUEUES

Queues consist of all the PNRs which require action from travel agent. It will have all the PNRs which have received replies by Airline in a sorted categorised way.

PNRs are placed in queue automatically as per reply by airline. PNRs will remain in Queue till appropriate action is taken on PNR or till PNR is purged from system.

It is definitely possible to place/delete PNR on Queue manually

QTQ command shows Queue Count with list of queues that exist on your office id and count of PNRs that exist in each queue

QT command is used to work on Queues and extract PNR to view /take action.

QI command is used to come out of Queue mode , it means exit Queue.

D1 today plus 2 days

D2 3rd day – 5th day

D3 6th day – 8th day

D4 9th day and beyond

Q1 Confirmation- It consist of PNRs which have received revert from Airline related to flight segments

Queue no	Category No	Date Range
Q1 CONFIRMATION	C1 AIR ITINERARY	D1
		D2
		D3
		D4
	C2 SSR	D1
		D2
		D3
		D4
	C7 OPW	D1
		D2
		D3
		D4
	C8 OPC	D1
		D2
		D3
		D4

To start Queue & view PNRs which received revert by Airline for flight segment which consists of departure of today, **Command is QS1C1D1**

To start Queue & view PNRs which have ticketing time limited issued by Airline for tomorrow,
Command is QS1C7D1
Q2 Waitlist – it consist of PNRs created on waitlist

Q8 TKTL – It consist of PNRs which have time limit applied by travel agent in TK element

Q2 & Q8 consist of just 1 category specific to that particular element only.

Q7 Schedule Change – it consist of PNRs in which there is change of time/ flight number/date in any flight segment by the Airline

Queue no	Category No
Q7Schedule Change	C0 (departure date of today)
	C1 (departure date of tomorrow)
	C2 (departure date of 2nd day from today)
	C3 (departure date of 3rd day from today) … … C14 (departure of 14th day from today)

You may make changes in PNR in Queue mode or you may just view the PNR in Queue mode, note down the PNR number, open in other command page and make required changes in PNR. Once appropriate action is taken in PNR, PNR will not be visible in that specific Queue. However if PNR requires more actions in any other element, PNR will definitely reflect in that specific queue no.

For example, a PNR received revert of KK on Air segment and NO in SSR, if you take appropriate action in Air Segment PNR will get removed from Q1 C1 but PNR will remain in Q1C6 as appropriate action is still required for SSR.

Sometimes C0 category is created by system automatically. If it consists of PNRs, then PNRs must be checked when working on Queues.

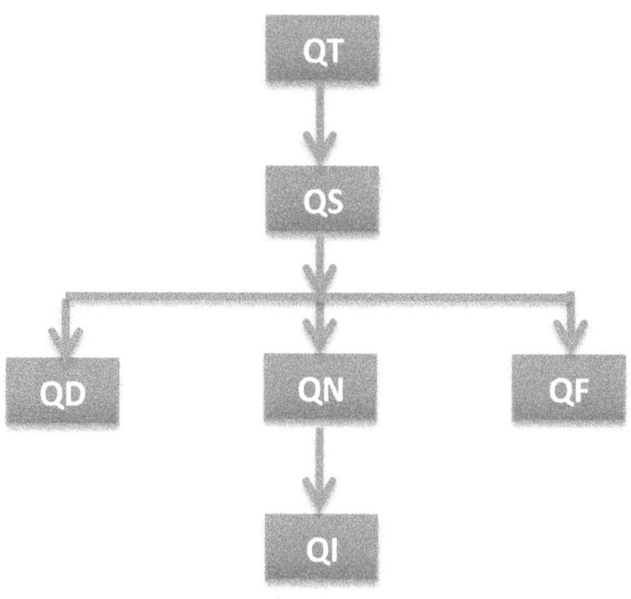

Command	
QN	Will remove the displayed PNR from queue & shows next PNR in sequence
QD	Will delay & keep the displayed PNR in queue & shows next PNR in sequence
QI	Will exit from Queue Mode
QF	If you made changes in PNR in queue mode. QF will save the changes & exit from queue mode

A TO Z OF AIR TICKETING

A – Search for AVAILABILITY of itinerary

B- BLOCK the seat

C- CONFIRM the PNR by adding

D- DETAILS of passenger

E –EMAIL itinerary to passenger

F – FILE the FARE

G – Generate GUARANTEED fare

H – HOLD the fare

I – check for INCOMING vendor remaks

J- ensure to price the JOURNEY as through ticket on single plating carrier

K – if you are holding lowest KLASS else told lowest KLASS to take lowes fare

L- LIST down the SSR you wish for

M – add MANDATORY fare modifiers

N- add NET REMIT CODE if you have

O- add OPTIONAL TOUR CODE if you have

P- add PASSPORT DETAILS of passengers

Q – QUEUE this pnr for ticket issuance

R- READ RULES of ticket like REISSUE, REFUND etc

S- check STATUS OF itinerary should be HK

T- issue TICKET

U- if coupon status of ETKT is U, it means ticket is unavailable . If Ochanges are allowed

V- if ticket is VOIDED then status of ETKT should change to V

W- for cancellations by airline/by agent, if you have WAIVER CODE, apply for full refund , reissue else

X- XANCELLATION charges will apply

Y- Y coupon status on ETKT means only taxes can be refunded

Z- Z coupon status on ETKT means ticket is closed & no changes can take place now

www.ingramcontent.com/pod-product-compliance
Lightning Source LLC
Chambersburg PA
CBHW040217110726
48005CB00019B/3054